M IS FOR
MYSTICAL

A Book for Mini Mystics

Written by **EMMA MILDON**

Illustrated by **SARA UGOLOTTI**

RP KIDS
PHILADELPHIA

Running Press Kids
Hachette Book Group
1290 Avenue of the Americas, New York, NY 10104
www.runningpress.com/rpkids
@runningpresskids

Distributed in the United Kingdom by Little, Brown Book Group UK,
Carmelite House, 50 Victoria Embankment, London, EC4Y 0DZ

Printed in China

First Edition: March 2024

Published by Running Press Kids, an imprint of Perseus Books, LLC, a subsidiary of Hachette Book Group, Inc. The Running Press Kids name and logo are trademarks of the Hachette Book Group.

The Hachette Speakers Bureau provides a wide range of authors for speaking events. To find out more, go to www.hachettespeakersbureau.com or email HachetteSpeakers@hbgusa.com.

Running Press books may be purchased in bulk for business, educational, or promotional use. For more information, please contact your local bookseller or the Hachette Book Group Special Markets Department at Special.Markets@hbgusa.com.

The publisher is not responsible for websites (or their content) that are not owned by the publisher.

Print book cover and interior design by Mary Boyer.

Library of Congress Cataloging-in-Publication Data
Names: Mildon, Emma, author. | Ugolotti, Sara, 1988- illustrator.
Title: M is for mystical: a book for mini mystics/written by Emma Mildon; illustrated by Sara Ugolotti.
Description: Philadelphia: RP/Kids, [2024] | Audience: Ages 5-9 | Summary: "A nonfiction, alphabet picture book that introduces young readers to New Age/mystical concepts"—Provided by publisher.
Identifiers: LCCN 2022050500 (print) | LCCN 2022050501 (ebook) | ISBN 9780762482610 (hardcover) | ISBN 9780762482627 (epub) | ISBN 9780762485130 (kindle edition) | ISBN 9780762485147 (nook edition)
Subjects: LCSH: Mysticism—Juvenile literature. | Alphabet books.
Classification: LCC B828 .M53 2024 (print) | LCC B828 (ebook) | DDC 149/.3—dc23/eng/20230310
LC record available at https://lccn.loc.gov/2022050500
LC ebook record available at https://lccn.loc.gov/2022050501
ISBNs: 978-0-7624-8261-0 (hardcover), 978-0-7624-8262-7 (ebook),
978-0-7624-8513-0 (ebook), 978-0-7624-8514-7 (ebook)

1010

10 9 8 7 6 5 4 3 2 1

For my daughters, Ada and Elin,
May your worlds be full of magic and wonder.

A IS FOR ASTROLOGY.

When you were born, the stars aligned. Astrology is the study of the planets and stars and how they affect our lives— from our actions and feelings to even how well we sleep.

Fun Fact: People have been guided by the stars since the start of time—kings, queens, sailors, and philosophers used astrology to help them navigate big decisions in life.

Exercise: Discover your place in the stars! Use the time of year you were born to determine your astrological sign.

March 21–April 19
ARIES | Ram
Brave, honest, passionate

April 20–May 20
TAURUS | Bull
Patient, stable, driven

May 21–June 21
GEMINI | Twins
Curious, affectionate, gentle

June 22–July 22
CANCER | Crab
Loyal, sympathetic, imaginative

July 23–August 2
LEO | Lion
Creative, generous, cheerful

August 23–September 22
VIRGO | Virgin
Kind, practical, hard working

September 23–October 23
LIBRA | Balance
Social, gracious, peace maker

October 24–November 21
SCORPIO | Scorpion
Passionate, brave, private

November 22–December 21
SAGITTARIUS | Archer
Funny, generous, idealistic

December 22–January 19
CAPRICORN | Goat
Responsible, focused, disciplined

January 20–February 18
AQUARIUS | Water Bearer
Clever, independent, kind

February 19–March 20
PISCES | Fish
Artistic, wise, compassionate

B IS FOR BREATH WORK.

Taking deep breaths helps us relax. When we breathe, we fill our lungs with oxygen that helps fuel our body.

Fun Fact: Your lungs are busy! Did you know you take around 20,000 breaths a day?

Exercise: Take a deep breath in through your nose. Hold it in for a few seconds and then blow out (exhale) through your mouth. Repeat. Consider this breath work a superpower you can use to help breathe away any worries.

C IS FOR CRYSTALS.

Crystals are gems and stones that have been used over centuries to bring good energy, offer healing, and help us manage our feelings. Depending on the type of crystal, its power can help with all sorts of things.

Fun Fact: Did you know crystals help power our phones, TVs, computers, and watches?

⇒ AMETHYST ⇐
Calm

⇒ TIGER'S-EYE ⇐
Confidence

⇒ CITRINE ⇐
Creativity

⇒ ROSE QUARTZ ⇐
Love

⇒ CLEAR QUARTZ ⇐
Healing

⇒ BLUE LACE AGATE ⇐
Communication

D IS FOR DREAMS.

Sleep is when we rest our minds and bodies, which allows us to recharge, restore, and reenergize. When you dream during sleep, you can have fun adventures—from flying and dancing to traveling the world or even space.

Fun Fact: The average person spends approximately six years of their life dreaming.

Exercise: Did you know you can daydream too? Close your eyes and imagine a world that is special for you. What do you see?

E IS FOR ESSENTIAL OILS.

Essential oils are made from different parts of plants—flowers, leaves, bark. Natural herbs, flowers, incense, oils, and perfumes are all part of the fragrant world of aromatherapy. Add a few drops of essential oil to your bath, pillow, or make a potion that smells great!

Fun Fact: The first of your five senses to develop is your ability to smell!

Exercise: Different herbs and flowers can help you in lots of ways.

⇾ LAVENDER ⇽
Reduces anxiety, calms, helps with sleep.

⇾ PEPPERMINT ⇽
Increases alertness, memory, focus.

⇾ LEMON ⇽
Improves mood, reduces anxiety.

⇾ LEMONGRASS ⇽
Repels insects, relieves stress.

⇾ EUCALYPTUS ⇽
Clears the airways, supports migraines and headaches.

⇾ BERGAMOT ⇽
Balances emotions, helps inflammation.

F IS FOR FAIRIES.

Did you know there are lots of types of fairies? These tiny, winged beings can often be found by streams, in gardens, hiding behind rocks, or in caves. Some are troublemakers while others are playful.

Fun Fact: You'll likely get a visit from a fairy one day; she goes by the name of the Tooth Fairy.

Exercise: Build your own fairy garden to welcome friendly fairies. They love flowers, water, honey, coins, and crystals.

G IS FOR GURU.

A guru is a teacher or guide. They can help you explore life, understand your emotions, and become your best self.

Fun Fact: Did you know you have a guru already? Your grown-ups, siblings, teachers, even your neighbors all help teach and guide you, just like a guru!

Exercise: Think about the people in your life who help you learn and grow. We discover so much every day. Draw a picture of them and the lesson they taught you and gift it to your guru.

H IS FOR HAND MUDRAS.

Hand mudras are special gestures that can help us focus or calm our minds. Yup, holding your hands in certain shapes can help give you superpower energy!

Fun Fact: Hand mudras have been proven to engage the brain.

Exercise: Practice making namaste mudra. Simply place your hands together palm-to-palm in front of your chest. This gives you the superpower of balance. Neat, huh?!

I IS FOR INCENSE.

Incense is a scented smoke that is burned in rituals, healings, and for meditation.

Fun Fact: Sandalwood incense has been said to make you feel happy and rid you of worry.

Exercise: You don't always need actual smoke to take away your worries. Wave your hands in the air around yourself like incense smoke would move. Imagine the air around you feeling lighter and happier.

→ **SANDALWOOD** ←

Brings good energy and happiness to a space.

→ **BERGAMOT** ←

Brings joy and balance to a space.

→ **FRANKINCENSE** ←

Supports emotions and balances mood.

→ **JASMINE** ←

Quiets the mind for restful sleep.

→ **PALO SANTO** ←

Provides protection.

→ **ROSE** ←

Brings love to a space.

→ **WHITE SAGE** ←

Purifies a space.

→ **JUNIPER** ←

Aids healing and calms the body.

J IS FOR JOY.

Joy is when you have great happiness. When you have the biggest smile ear-to-ear and feel cheerful and content. You can find joy in lots of things in your day. From the sun shining on you or just by celebrating things you learn and experience.

Fun Fact: Feeling joy helps your body be happy and healthy.

**Exercise: Draw a picture of something that brings you joy—
your friends, flowers, the beach, swings, even your pet.**

K IS FOR KUNDALINI.

Kundalini is an energy, also called Shakti, which lays asleep in all of us. Practices like Kundalini Yoga help us explore this energy through yoga poses, meditation, chanting, singing, breathing exercises, and our imagination.

Fun Fact: Kundalini is sometimes shown as a coiled snake that, when awakened, moves through us giving us power. Super snake!

Exercise: Make fists with both your hands and point your index fingers up. As you chant the following mantra, keep your fingers pointed up and shake your hands while singing:

"I AM HAPPY, I AM GOOD, I AM HAPPY, I AM GOOD.
SAT NAAM, SAT NAAM, SAT NAAM JEE.
WHA-HAY GUROO, WHA-HAY GUROO,
WHA-HAY GUROO JEE."

Repeat for a few minutes and see how you are feeling!

L IS FOR LUNAR CYCLE.

Lunar cycles are when the moon goes through its eight main phases. It takes approximately 29.5 days to complete a cycle. Each stage of the moon affects us differently.

Fun Fact: The moon is the second brightest thing in the sky after the sun.

Exercise: What moon do you see in the sky?

> **NEW MOON** <
A time for new beginnings.

> **WAXING CRESCENT MOON** <
A time for hope and positivity.

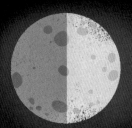

> **FIRST QUARTER MOON** <
A time for action and decisions.

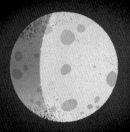

> **WAXING GIBBOUS MOON** <
A time for reflection.

> **FULL MOON** <
A time for letting go.

> **WANING GIBBOUS MOON** <
A time for gratitude.

> **LAST QUARTER MOON** <
A time for forgiving and moving forward.

> **WANING CRESCENT MOON** <
A time for stillness and peace.

M IS FOR MYSTICAL.

The mystical world is about magic, spirituality, and looking for hidden meanings and deeper understanding in life.

Fun Fact: Children's natural curiosity and sense of magic and wonder often mean they are more in tune with the mystical world.

Exercise: Let's do a mystic meditation and take a mindful walk. First, grow still, close your eyes, and take a deep breath in and out. Open your eyes and move slowly and silently. What magic do you see, hear, or feel?

N IS FOR NATURE.

We are so lucky to get to share our world with plants and animals. Nature teaches us strength, unity, connection, and harmony. Getting outside and surrounding ourselves with nature can help us become more mindful and aware of the world around us.

Fun Fact: Ladybugs are nature's gardeners; they eat little bugs that harm plants.

Exercise: Get out in nature and explore all the things you hear, see, smell, and feel. Visit a local park, plant some flower pots at home, or venture out to the forest.

O IS FOR OBSERVATION.

We can learn a lot from watching and listening. Observation makes you more aware of everything around you—how you and others may feel, sounds, colors, and smells. There are lots of ways to observe—you can meditate, listen, or write down things you see, experience, and feel.

Fun Fact: Some people can actually feel other people's thoughts and emotions. Empaths observe other people's energy and absorb it themselves. When other people are sad, they are sad for them, and when others are happy, empaths feel that happiness, too.

Exercise: Play I-spy with your family and see what feelings you can observe in each other.

P IS FOR PALM READING.

Palm reading uses the lines on the palm of your hand to determine your personality and predict your future. Palmistry studies the shape and size of a hand, as well as mounts and lines.

Fun Fact: Do you have big or small hands? Big palms mean you like facts, prefer the quiet, and like taking time to think things over. While smaller palms mean you are likely to be a decision maker and have fun being with your friends.

Exercise: Lots of mini mystics tend to have lines in the shape of the letter M on their palm. Do you have an M? It can signify your ability to manifest and create magic.

Q IS FOR QUESTIONS.

Asking questions and being interested in new things can help you learn and grow and is what Mysticism is all about! Answers come from asking . . .

Fun Fact: Did you know four-year-olds ask around 300 questions a day?!

Exercise: Ask three questions today. They can be about anything—what a person dreamt that night, why the grass is green, or what someone's favorite animal is!

R IS FOR RITUAL.

A ritual is a ceremony of actions that symbolize something. Rituals can be for worship or celebration.

Fun Fact: Lighting birthday candles is an ancient ritual!
Today, it is one of the most popular rituals in the world.

Exercise: What is something you can do every day to help bring more magic to your life? Make this a new morning ritual. It can be something simple like writing down a word you want to focus on, like joy, calm, play, or focus.

S IS FOR SPIRIT GUIDES.

Spirit guides can be animals, insects, angels, and departed loved ones. They help protect and guide you in life.

Fun Fact: Animal guides have special meanings in ancient Greek, Native American, Chinese, and African cultures.

Exercise: Signs from your guides can include a butterfly, a feather, a song, or repeating numbers. Draw or write down the different signs you come across each day.

T IS FOR TAROT.

Tarot decks are made up of seventy-eight cards that give us insights into our life. Different cards have different pictures and meanings.

Fun Fact: Tarot was originally a 14th-century card game, not a tool for fortune telling.

Exercise: Turn tarot into a daily game! Each day pull a new card and talk about what you see. Animal cards are perfect for this type of ritual, as you can pretend to be whatever animal your card shows—brave like a lion, fast like a rabbit, etc.

U IS FOR THE UNIVERSE.

The universe is a name for the world above us. It is full of lots of magical things like galaxies, stars, space, and planets, as well as things we haven't seen or discovered yet.

Fun Fact: There are more stars than grains of sand on the beach.

Exercise: Draw your very own universe. It can have rockets, planets, special stars, your family, pets, and friends. Expand your world!

V IS FOR VALUES.

Our values are the things we believe in or the things that are most important to us. Values like honesty, kindness, sharing, forgiveness, and friendship all say a lot about who we are as a person.

Fun Fact: Everyone's values are different! It's important to respect everyone's values, especially those close to us.

☑ KINDNESS
☑ SHARING
☑ MANNERS
☑ HONESTY
☑ FAMILY
☑ LEARNING
☑ PLAY

Exercise: Make a list of the values that are most important to you or your family. Here are some ideas to get your list started: Kindness. Sharing. Manners. Honesty. Family. Learning. Play . . .

W IS FOR WISDOM.

Wisdom can come from things we read, are told, or that we experience. The lessons we encounter in life help us understand the difference between right and wrong.

Fun Fact: Being smart isn't the same as being wise. Being wise is when we think before we do or say something.

Exercise: Let's think about something that happened to you this week that you learned from. Share an experience, mistake, or challenge that helped you become wiser.

X IS FOR EXPLORATION.

Exploration leads to new discoveries and is one of the most important things about mystic living. Animals, nature, people, places can all teach us something if we are open to exploring the world around us. Ask questions, listen, observe.

Fun Fact: Exploration doesn't always require going somewhere—it can be as simple as trying a new food.

Exercise: Make a list of places you want to explore or new things you want to try!

Y IS FOR YIN AND YANG.

Yin and Yang is the Chinese symbol for balance. It teaches us that everything in the world has an opposite, but together they make a whole. Like day and night— separately, one is light and the other is dark, but together they make a whole day.

Fun Fact: The Yin Yang sign is a circle split by a curved line that has one dark side and one light side. Within these halves is a dot of the opposite color, showing contrast, completeness, and harmony.

Exercise: Let's play Yin & Yang Yoga. Alternate a slow pose then a fast-moving action.

Yin yoga poses (hold for ten seconds):
happy baby, child's pose, or caterpillar.

Yang movements (move for ten seconds): star jumps, running
on the spot, or reaching high and then touching your toes.

Z IS FOR ZEN.

Zen is the Buddhist art of meditating and relaxing so much you learn to control your thoughts and not overreact to things.

Fun Fact: Zen is an ancient practice with roots to India, China, and Japan and is the art of thinking of nothing.

Exercise: The next time you feel frustrated, upset, or angry, take a moment to think about what you are feeling and why. Take a deep breath in and out and find your calm again. Even just counting your breath—1, 2, 3 can help you calm down and find zen!